C000163556

TRANSFORMATIONAL BUSINESS NETWORK

Fighting Poverty Through Enterprise
The case for Social Venture Capital

Brian Griffiths and Kim Tan

Transformational Business Network
Nelson House – 271 Kingston Road – Wimbledon
London – SW19 3NW

ISBN No. 978-1-909886-18-6

Third Edition Published by
Anchor Recordings Ltd
72 The Street
Kennington
Ashford Kent
TN24 9 HS

Printed in UK by CreateSpace

CONTENTS

INTRODUCTION

To date, the debate on tackling global poverty has been dominated by the case for greater aid. We believe that foreign aid has a role and support the target of 0.7% being given by rich countries to developing countries. However, we have written this paper because we believe that much greater emphasis needs to be given to the part that business and enterprise can play in reducing poverty. In recent years China and India are dramatic examples of countries which have reformed their economies, opened them up to trade and investment, embraced an enterprise culture, and lifted millions of their citizens out of poverty. Despite its dismal record over many years we believe that Africa has the same potential as Asia.

We believe that funds transferred from developed to developing countries are more effective in creating permanent jobs if they are made as investments, seeking financial and social returns, rather than as government- to-government grants. In this context micro-credit has been a crucial first step in directly helping the poor escape poverty. The case we wish to argue in this paper is that social venture capital has the potential to become a new asset class and a critical second step to support the growth of small and medium sized enterprises in developing countries, so creating jobs and reducing poverty.

CHAPTER 1

The scar on our conscience

Nearly 50% of the world's population – almost 3 billion people – live on less than $2 a day. 840 million suffer from hunger. Ten million children die every year from easily preventable diseases. AIDS kills 3 million people every year and is spreading. One billion people lack access to sanitation. One billion adults are illiterate. About one-quarter of children in poor countries do not finish primary school. Meanwhile the richest 20% of the world's population own 77% of the world's wealth while the poorest 20% own 1.4%.

Statistics such as these present two problems: First, they make the problem of poverty, disease and hunger impersonal. It is impossible to imagine the human pain, deprivation and suffering when presented with numbers alone. Statistics simply cannot convey the despair which poor people feel which is why the World Bank's three volume study Voices of the Poor was such a significant publication. Second, there is the scale of the problem. How can we come to terms with hundreds of millions of people suffering each day from hunger? Or thousands of children, let alone millions, dying each year from preventable diseases? The problems that statistics describe are so vast as to seem insurmountable with the result that people feel incapable of motivating themselves 'yet again' to think about the poor, never mind tackling global poverty. Such difficulties are often compounded by hearing accounts of failed aid projects, the creaming-off of funds by corrupt government leaders and the flight of capital (especially from Africa). Because of the scale of the problem individuals feel powerless to help and so the temptation is to offer a token response without any real involvement or commitment.

It is important to affirm that the poverty of Africa is 'a scar on our conscience'. Whatever our moral compass global poverty is a scandalous state of affairs. What makes it even worse is that for problems such as the easily preventable deaths of children, access to clean water and universal primary education, there are ways to help which do not involve great expense. In view of the disparity in wealth between rich countries and poor countries it is impossible to escape the conclusion that tackling poverty is a responsibility rich countries must accept.

Quite apart from the moral argument, however, is the fact that continued economic divergence between Africa and the rest of the world is both socially and politically unsustainable. In 1960, per capita income in Africa and East Asia were roughly the same. By 2004, GDP per capita in East Asian countries was five times higher than in Africa. If we measure the difference, even adjusting for purchasing power parity, then in 1960 African incomes per capita were just over two-thirds of those of East Asia and the Pacific, but by 2000 they were less than one-quarter. Such a divergence in income between poor and wealthier countries will inevitably put greater pressure on illegal migration out of Africa as well as the export of drugs and criminal activity to the rest of the world. In addition, while poverty is not a direct cause of terrorism it nevertheless provides a fertile breeding ground for disaffected and unemployed young people with no hope of improving their circumstances.

It is because of these factors that the need to tackle global poverty has been increasingly recognised by governments and NGOs. In the run up to the Millennium, the Jubilee 2000 campaign was highly successful in cancelling third world debt. Then in 2000 189 countries signed up to the Millennium Development Goals (MDGs), namely to:

(i)   eradicate extreme poverty and hunger,
(ii)   provide primary schools for all children,
(iii) empower women and promote gender equality,

(iv)   reduce child mortality,

(v)   improve maternal health,

(vi)   fight HIV/AIDS, malaria and other diseases,

(vii)   ensure environmental sustainability and,

(viii) promote global partnerships for development … all by the year 2015.

Because of the particular problems of Africa the UK government set up a commission which issued a Report on Africa in 2004, and then in 2005, during the UK's chairmanship of the G8, made poverty reduction in Africa one of its two key agenda items. To lobby the G8 countries to do more in 2005 Bob Geldof and Bono put on the 'Live 8' concerts as part of the 'Make Poverty History' campaign. At the 2005 Gleneagles Summit, the G8 countries committed to further cancellation of third world debt, improving free trade through the Doha round and doubling the volume of aid to Africa. In 2006, the UK, along with six other European countries, established a new development agency, IFFIm, and launched a highly successful $1 billion dollar bond to fund immunisation and vaccination.

The recent UK government White Paper Eliminating World Poverty noted that global poverty is falling overall. The rapid economic growth in Asia means that the number of people in the world living on less than US $1 dollar a day is set to halve by 2015. As further good news the report also observed that over 75 million more children attend primary school than in 1990. However, the distribution of poverty alleviation is far from even, as the report went on to say:

> Most of the improvements have been in Asia, particularly in East Asia. Some countries in sub-Saharan Africa are making progress, but the region as a whole will not meet any of the MDGs; and South Asia is off-track on education, health, water and sanitation. Across both regions, the spread of AIDS, malaria, tuberculosis and

other diseases continues to present a major challenge. Progress has also been slow in other regions, such as Latin America and Central Asia – but the absolute numbers of poor people there remain low compared to South Asia and sub-Saharan Africa. On current trends, by 2015 over 90% of the world's poor will live in sub-Saharan Africa and South Asia.

CHAPTER 2

Why aid is never enough

For the past five decades the major approach by governments to tackle global poverty has been through government to government aid. Foreign aid as we have known it over recent decades started with President Truman's Four Point Programme outlined in his inaugural address of January 1949:

> We must embark on a bold new programme for … the improvement and growth of underdeveloped areas. More than half the people of the world are living in conditions approaching misery … For the first time in history, humanity possesses the knowledge and the skill to relieve the suffering of the people.

Since then William Easterly, formerly a World Bank economist, estimates that US $2.3 trillion has been given in aid. Richard Dowden, director of the Royal Africa Society, estimates that in the last fifty years Africa has received around US $1 trillion, or roughly US $5,000 for every African living today if it were distributed evenly at today's prices. Some have agreed that because of the success of the Marshall Plan, extended by the US to help Europe recover from the Second World War, there should today be the equivalent of a Marshall Plan for Africa. However, Bowden estimates that over the past fifty years aid extended to Africa has been roughly the equivalent of six Marshall Plans. Yet aid is still seen as the core element of UK policy.

Frequently, donor governments and aid agencies demonstrate their commitment to tackle global poverty by the volume of aid they provide. But this is to confuse what we could call 'inputs' and 'outputs'. The amount of aid given is an 'input' to development. The 'outputs' are poverty reduction, provision of schooling, improvements in health and so on. The major reason aid has been subject to so much criticism is not because of the shortfall in volume (input) but because of its ineffectiveness in terms of output.

Four criticisms stand out in particular:

The *first* is that aid encourages inefficiency and waste. Much aid money has been squandered on prestigious projects that have not contributed to economic growth or poverty alleviation but simply allowed local politicians to 'skim off' money for themselves.

Second, is the charge that aid distorts the local economies. Poor countries do not have the capacity to absorb a huge inflow of aid dollars. When large amounts of aid money is spent on local goods and services, it has the unintentional effect of increasing the real exchange rates of countries and increasing money supply and inflation rates that could end up hurting the very people whom the aid policies are designed to help. Even when aid is delivered in the form of goods from donor countries, from food to shelters, it can affect the local suppliers as a result of 'dumping'.

Third, aid can empower Third Word governments to pursue perverse political agendas because foreign aid is government-to-government. The negative consequences of such policies include land grabs, 'villagisation' of agriculture ending with reduced food production, subsidising of national airlines and the barbarism of ethnic cleansing. As *the Journal of the Institute of Economic Affairs* noted in December 2003,

> Most aid still goes to corrupt governments. National and international aid bureaucracies, in alliance with assorted consultants, academics and NGOs, have a vested interest in the aid business, mostly with little regards to policy results.

Finally, it has not proved possible in economic research to find any reliable relationship between aid and economic growth. For example, aid to Africa increased throughout the 1990s from 5% of GDP to 17% of GDP. Yet GDP growth actually decreased from 2% to zero or negative growth *(World Bank Development Indicators, 2003).* Neither is there any clear demonstrable relationship between aid and poverty reduction.

The World Bank has estimated that 60% of all foreign aid stays within donor countries, and is used to pay for consultants to purchase nationally produced goods and for transportation costs. The late Indian Prime Minister Rajiv Ghandi conjectured that less than 15 cents in the dollar in aid gets to the poor beneficiaries. The charitable, NGO and philanthropic sector in the USA alone is an annual US $240 billion industry. This is a huge 'Third Sector' with vested interests in the aid business and with money and institutional interests at stake.

In their influential paper published in 2000, World Bank economists, Burnside and Dollar showed that 'aid has a positive impact on growth in developing countries with good fiscal, monetary and trade policies, *but has little effect in the presence of poor policies.'* Their first conclusion, that aid has a positive impact in countries with good policies (low budget deficits, low inflation, free trade), suggested that aid should not be given across the board but focussed on those countries with good policies. It was on this basis that the US set up the Millennium Challenge Corporation with extra funding and developed sixteen indicators of what constituted good policies. However, using new data for a longer time period and more data from the original period Easterly, Levine and Roodman found that there was no evidence that aid even raised growth among countries with good policies. Their second conclusion, after 50 years of aid, is surely self-evident: historical evidence suggests that good governance and policies help economies grow and reduce poverty *whether they receive aid or not.* In other words, when countries have good policies and governance, they really do not need aid.

The late Peter Bauer devoted most of his academic life to exposing the flaws and failures of foreign aid after having lived in and studied the rubber industry in Malaya (now Malaysia) and the problems of primary producers and trade in West Africa. In 1998 to mark the fiftieth anniversary of the inception of foreign aid, he wrote (with Cranley Onslow) an essay entitled *Fifty Years of Failure*. His conclusion was that foreign aid had not only not helped, but had positively harmed the poor in developing countries. It encouraged inefficiency and waste, and the adoption of perverse policies by governments of developing countries. His recommendation was simple: government-to- government hand-outs should be ended.

Professor Jeffrey Sachs has been one of the key champions for increasing the volume of aid to Africa. In his Millennium Villages project, Sachs proposed three steps out of rural poverty, first an increase in food production, next an improvement in healthcare and education, and finally participation in international trade. He argued that because of the corruption and 'skimming' of aid dollars and the piecemeal effort of government and NGO initiatives, too little aid actually gets through to the poor, and when it does it is uncoordinated and badly executed. He called for targeted aid to boost food production in order to overcome the cycles of famine and achieve improvement in healthcare. But it is clear that Sachs is also calling for an increase in economic activities in terms of manufactured goods and services that can be traded internationally. Even sceptics of foreign aid can see some rationale to Sachs' 'triple transformation' approach. Areas such as healthcare and education are clearly best addressed by governments and NGOs. However, we disagree that this is the right approach for agricultural production and manufacturing or service activities. These activities are best initiated and managed in partnership with private enterprises using commercial capital, but not run by governments and NGOs.

Debt Cancellation

One particular form of aid is the cancellation of the foreign debt of poor countries. As a result of the Jubilee 2000 campaign, the G8 countries together with the IMF and World Bank launched the Highly Indebted Poor Countries (HIPC) debt restructuring initiative. This has led to the cancellation of over US $60 billion of debt from 26 countries.

Debt cancellation has had its critics. The main issue is whether the cancellation of debts will lead to further irresponsible behaviour by political leaders in Highly Indebted Poor Countries. Will the money saved from interest payments be used wisely by these leaders in the interests of their people? These are valid concerns and yet a number of points need to be made. First, debt restructuring occurs every day between banks and corporations. In many instances, and as part of the restructuring, there is an element of debt cancellation. Bad debts that are irrecoverable have to be cancelled in order that companies are able to restructure. Is there any difference between this and bad debts owed by sovereign states? Second, debt cancellation can have conditionalities imposed on the debtor nation that significantly benefit the poor. In Tanzania and Burundi, money saved as a result of their debt relief programmes has been used successfully to provide universal free primary school education. Third, although debt cancellation is not a legal right of poor countries, it is a morally responsible action of donor countries. It is a fundamental need of poor countries, so that they can have a fresh start to do new things in the basic provision of education, health and shelter.

International Finance Facility for Immunisation (IFFIm)

One of the newest forms of aid is the International Financing Facility for Immunisation (IFFIm). In November 2006, a new multilateral development institution, (IFFIm), backed by the governments of France, Italy, Spain, Norway, Sweden and the UK, launched a highly successful US $1 billion bond issue which is the first step in raising US $4 billion over the next ten years. This year the governments of Brazil and South Africa intend to join IFFIm.

The objective of IFFIm is to save the lives of children. The funds raised are being used by GAVI, the Global Alliance for Vaccines and Immunisation to vaccinate 500 million children against diseases such as measles, tetanus and yellow fever in the 70 poorest countries of the world. GAVI expects this will prevent 5 million child deaths between now and 2015 and more than five million adult deaths in the future, a total saving of 10 million lives.

The complexity of the initiative – a 5-year AAA rated bond with a 5% coupon, priced just 31 basis points over a 5-year US Treasury bond, along with the creation of a new institution, the IFFIm, and the involvement of GAVI, which is itself only 6 years old – should not disguise either the simplicity or the significance of the initiative.

The idea is straightforward. Soon after the commitment to halving poverty and improving health education by 2015 was made at the UN Millennium Summit in 2000 it became clear that these goals would not be met, especially in sub-Saharan Africa. At the same time the governments of rich countries would continue providing aid for the foreseeable future. The proposal was to use these future commitments as collateral for raising funds now, so that the programme of vaccination and immunisation could be brought forward.

The real significance of IFFIm however is that it is a new approach to foreign aid.

It is not money given government-to-government. IFFIm is a registered UK charity with an independent board of directors. It is accountable to the Charity Commissioners, the governments which have pledged funds and the bond holders. It has promised to pay interest, to repay the principal and to issue regular financial statements. Similarly, the immunisation programme on the ground will be administered by GAVI, the brainchild of the Bill and Melinda Gates Foundation, who invested US $750 million to set it up and another US $750 million to its growth.

GAVI is not just an alliance of governments but a public private partnership of all the major stakeholders in immunisation, including permanent members (WHO, UNICEF, World Bank, the Bill and Melinda Gates Foundation), developing country and donor governments, vaccine companies, NGOs and research bodies. The 70 poorest countries in the world are to receive funds subject to only one condition, namely that they must not be in protracted arrears on their debt obligations to the IMF.

Unlike the traditional approach to aid, IFFlm and GAVI offer much greater transparency. They have made a commitment that 65 cents of every dollar raised will be spent to buy vaccines and 30 cents used to employ nurses, vehicles, refrigeration and strengthen health systems in poor countries, with the balance used for administration. Because of this IFFlm and GAVI are different from the World Bank. The World Bank raises debt on the international capital markets and uses the funds to make loans. GAVI by contrast is a remarkably transparent process and there are effective metrics by which to judge its performance.

Immunisation is an area where the metrics are very clear. The number of vaccinations can be easily measured. Similarly, indicators of success are straightforward: the under 5 mortality rate, the infant mortality rate, the number of children immunised against specific diseases. IFFlm has delegated to GAVI the process of auditing each programme and measuring its success, something again which is critical to the success of the venture.

IFFlm could well become the prototype for the new way aid is given in the future. The process is transparent and accountable and could be extended to other areas. There could be an IFFed to fund primary schools, literacy and numeracy programmes, an IFFwat to fund water projects and an IFFinf to fund infrastructure projects. The key to each would be a process which was transparent, where the lines of accountability were clear and where the impact of aid was measured not by how much money was given but by results. It would also disarm skeptics.

CHAPTER 3

Free trade and 'Fair Trade'

If developing countries are to grow more rapidly and reduce poverty they need access to the markets of developed countries. This has happened for the BRICs countries – Brazil, Russia, India and China. Their share of world trade (measured by imports plus exports as a percentage of world trade) has nearly doubled since 2003 driven largely by China. Poorer developing countries however face serious protectionist barriers for exports of agricultural products, cotton, steel and service.

Farm subsidies in the EU, the USA and Canada, and the USA's steel tariffs total over US $300 billion per year and are larger than the combined national income of Sub-Saharan Africa and dwarf the US $50 billion given in aid a year. To put it more starkly, the dairy subsidy in the EU is US $2.50 per cow per day whilst 2.8 billion people live on less than US $2 per day. In other words, European cows are worth more than half the world's poor.

Sadly sub-Saharan Africa's share of world trade declined from 6% in 1980 to only 2% in 2002. Interestingly intra-regional trade accounts for only 5% of GDP in Africa while in East Asia and the Pacific the figure is 27%.

The governments which signed the Doha Declaration of the World Trade Organisation (WTO) in 2001 sought to establish a fairer and less protected international trading system which in particular would benefit developing countries. Those countries which have successfully tackled poverty have also been those which have opened their countries to the rest of the world both in trade and foreign investment, opening up economies, encouraging competition and productivity and faster economic growth. The intention at Doha was to open up markets for agricultural products, textiles, clothing and services and reduce farm subsidies in the EU and US as well as export subsidies. In addition Aid for Trade and trade facilitation agreements would have helped poor countries adjust.

At the same time it was recognised at Doha that developing countries needed 'special and differential treatment' to protect their small farms when barriers are reduced and to reduce non-tariff barriers such as 'rule of origin' which prevent developing countries from paying inputs from the cheapest sources.

The failure of the WTO negotiations in Cancun (2003), Geneva (2004), Paris (2005), Hong Kong (2005) and Geneva (2006) has cast doubt over whether the goals of the Doha Declaration will ever be met. The talks have stalled over a major divide between the European Union and the United States and between them and the major G20 developing countries led by the G4 bloc (China, India, Brazil and South Africa). In essence, the US believes that Europe, Japan and India are not doing enough to open up their agricultural markets to services and lowering industrial tariffs. From a European perspective the US was not doing enough to reduce farm subsidies. Brazil wanted more concessions especially on agriculture from both the US and the EU, India wanted easier access to services in developed countries and Japan was reluctant to make further concessions on agriculture. Many obstacles remain to be negotiated before the Doha objectives of freer trade can be implemented. This, however, is just the kind of help the poor nations need. But it is the one help they may not get. The widespread belief in developing countries is that 'the West professes free trade but practises protectionism'.

A failure to agree even a modest settlement of the Doha round, such as some reduction in agricultural protection and services and a significant agreement on trade facilitation underpinned by Aid for Trade, has far more serious implications than just market access for developing countries. The real danger is that the world economy could slip back into a form of protectionism which produced such devastating consequences in the 1920s and 1930s and undermines the multi-lateral trading system which has developed since the founding of the GATT (precursor to the WTO) at the end of the Second World War. Already over 200 regional trade agreements have been notified to the WTO (which may simply direct trade rather than create trade) which could lead to great acrimony especially in terms of dealing with rules of origin for deciding whether preferential duties should be levied.

While trade liberalisation will certainly stimulate trade, developing countries must be in a position to take advantage of a more liberalised environment. Unless local people are effectively trained, encouraged and supported to get into business, they will be unable to benefit from the immense potential that increased trade has to offer. As the DIFD publication, Trade Matters comments:

> Supporting the continued reduction in trade barriers world-wide will not help developing countries greatly unless there is a simultaneous commitment to improve the capacity of those countries to take advantage of new trading opportunities which arise. (p. 22)

The 'Fair Trade' Movement

The 'Fair Trade' movement is made up of over 1/2 million small-scale producers and over 3000 grassroots organisations in 50 developing countries. The movement dates back to the 1940s when US churches began selling handicrafts made by refugees in Europe after World War II. Organisations such as Ten Thousand Villages in the Mennonite churches and SERRV International were early pioneers in offering higher returns to producers in the developing world through direct trade and fair prices.

Initially, fair trade products were sold through world-shops or fair trade charity shops. In order to generate greater sales on fair trade terms for the benefit of disadvantaged and marginalised producers, it was important to get fair trade into supermarkets where most people do their shopping. This has been achieved through a fair trade certification. As long as manufacturers agreed to buy from registered suppliers according to fair trade criteria their products could carry the fair trade seal of approval. In 1989, the Netherlands became the first country to launch the fair trade consumer guarantee – the Max Havelaar label. Today there are labelling initiatives in 20 countries, mainly throughout Europe and North America, and the product range now includes coffee, drinking chocolate, chocolate bars, orange juice, tea, honey, sugar, bananas, flowers and clothing. In the UK, the FAIRTRADE Mark is awarded by the Fairtrade Foundation which was set up by CAFOD, Christian Aid, Oxfam and Traidcraft. Today, products such as Café Direct and Tea Direct are established brands stocked by the major supermarket chains.

Fair trade sales were estimated at just over £1 billion in 2005 and represent just 1/100th of 1% of world trade in physical merchandise. But in certain product categories Fair trade sales in Europe and the US may reach 5% of the total.

But the fair trade movement is about more than trade. It is concerned with ensuring fair conditions for workers in the developing world who produce these products. It is about ensuring that there is no exploitation of wages, health and safety standards and transfer pricing in order that the poor producers are treated fairly. The Fair Trade Federation is an association of fair trade wholesalers, retailers, and producers whose members are committed to providing fair wages and employment opportunities to economically- disadvantaged artisans and farmers worldwide. The launch of the Red Label by Bono and a number of clothing chains where a percentage of the sales goes towards the producers are other examples of the working out of fair trade.

The gains from fair trade are insignificant compared to the gains from freer trade through Doha but fair trade is nevertheless an important step in showing that consumers in developed countries are committed to increasing trade while respecting the dignity of producers.

Fair trade has come in for legitimate criticism from market oriented economists because by attempting to set a minimum price floor (e.g. for coffee) above the world market price, it encourages producers to increase production which can only be sold at a lower price, thereby exacerbating the problem it was meant to solve. Far better, argue critics, is to encourage initiatives to boost demand, such as those in Brazil in the 1990s, or encourage coffee producers to move into higher value products in response to the growing speciality coffee market.

CHAPTER 4

Micro-credit as a first step

Western governments have committed themselves to helping the developing world through supporting Micro Enterprise Development (MED) in developing countries in order to facilitate sustainable development. To date it has proved difficult for the governments to focus effectively on MED, with its conflicting funding requirements.

For example, between 2000 and 2001, the UK's Department for International Development (DFID) dedicated just 4.8% of its budget to fund industry overseas. This is short-sighted and disappointing since MED has demonstrated its ability to help the poor achieve some self-reliance and dignity through economic activity.

One of the success stories in poverty reduction over the past 30 years has been the development of micro-finance institutions (MFIs) that provide small (a few hundred dollars) un-collateralised loans ('micro-credit') to poor entrepreneurs to start up micro-businesses. The loan repayment rate among MFIs is exceptionally high (usually greater than 90%) especially if loans are made to women rather than men.

Since its humble beginnings in 1971, when Opportunity International, a Christian not-for-profit organisation, began lending in Colombia, followed by ACCION International in 1973, microfinance has grown to a multi-billion dollar industry. In 2004, the International Finance Corporation (a subsidiary of the World Bank) through its partners had a combined loan portfolio of US $2.5 billion and over 1.3 million small entrepreneurs in developing countries.

The Grameen Bank which started in 1976 has become famous for its model of offering micro-credit to women in small groups. To qualify, Grameen's female customers have to earn less than a dollar a day. Group members are required to monitor each other at weekly meetings, applying varying degrees of pressure to ensure repayment. As loans are repaid, people are allowed to borrow more. The group in effect replaces the security that pawnshops gained from collateral. The model is not perfect, but it works and lifts people out of abject poverty. Such is the success that mainstream banking groups such as Citigroup and India's ICICI are now entering the market. This is a preferable way to assist the poor to become financially independent.

The advantages of MEDs are clear:

First, it is a low risk way to unlock the entrepreneurial skills of the poor – low risk for both lenders and borrowers. In all the developing countries, one can see the entrepreneurial talents of the poor by the road side as well as in their fruit, vegetable and fish markets. There is a huge latent entrepreneurial pool that can be released through MED.

Second, the impact is immediate in that the poor can start where they are with no new skills needed. There is no formal training to acquire new skills or technical expertise.

Third, it is one of the best solutions for income security for the poor. MEDs enable the poor to start small businesses that increase their daily income immediately.

Finally, it moves the poor from a welfare dependency mentality which in turns leads to individual responsibility and dignity for the poor.

For all its merits, there are limitations to MED. This is because the primary role of MED is poverty alleviation, not enterprise creation. MED is the fastest and best way to lift people out of abject poverty into 'normal' poverty, but they are still poor. As sole proprietors with small loans, there will always be physical and financial limitations on expansion of their businesses. The success of MEDs has been due largely to targeting the loans at women. This however can also be a limitation. The culture of the developing countries unfortunately still views women as home makers and not as business people. In fairness, the women who take on micro-credit loans do it primarily to boost their family income rather than as a means to build enterprises for themselves. There has been little evidence of progression from micro-credit to establishing fully registered businesses. According to Dr Vinay Samuel of The Bridge Foundation (India) it is estimated that only 3-5% of people with micro – credit move upwards to establish higher levels of income. However, he believes at least 10 – 20% of these have the skill sets to move into small and medium size enterprises. The Bridge Foundation's experience is that MEDs are flat cycles with very little spiralling upwards into scalable enterprises. Undoubtedly, MED can help reduce the debt burden of the poor at the hands of money lenders who charge exorbitant interest rates. Those who criticise MFIs for charging over 50% interest rates per annum for lending to the poor ought to compare this to the extortionate rates charged by loan sharks.

However, with such small amounts of money and little other support, training or investment, only a few among the poor can expect to succeed as entrepreneurs. Added to this is the widespread practise of multiple borrowings to service existing loans. In the same way that consumers in the West borrow on one credit card to pay the loans on another, many beneficiaries of micro-credit repay the loan from income received from their regular jobs, from grants provided by government for self-help programmes and from other MFIs. Not surprisingly, it is the intermediaries – the commercial banks and MFIs – who stand to gain the most from the spread between the cost of funds and loan interest rates. Undoubtedly, micro-credit has a vital role to play because it enables the poor to pay off expensive debts and manage their cash flow. However, its role in stimulating upward mobility of the poor into enterprise remains to be developed.

CHAPTER 5

The case for Social Venture Capital

Apart from micro-finance there is also a growing movement to use business enterprise to tackle global poverty. As the UK governments White Paper on *Eliminating World Poverty* noted, 'It is the private sector – from farmers and street traders to foreign investors that creates growth. Growth is fuelled by the creativity and hard work of entrepreneurs and workers.' This movement has grown out of entrepreneurs using the same skills and expertise that have enabled them to build successful businesses and applying their talents and resources to the problem of poverty.

We call this approach Social Venture Capital (Social VC) or social enterprise. So what is social venture capital? These are for-profit social venture funds investing in small-medium-size enterprises (SMEs) in developing countries. They take an enterprise approach to poverty alleviation by building commercially sustainable companies that create jobs and empower the poor to improve their livelihoods. They adopt the principles, discipline and accountability of venture capital investing but with a sub-venture capital rate of financial returns.

Henry Ford once said: 'A business that only makes money is a poor kind of business'. Most businesses exist solely to make a profit for their shareholders – that is the financial bottom line. Social VC looks beyond just financial returns to social and environmental returns as well. Social Venture Capital therefore is not investing purely for a financial return. That is not to say that it is in it to lose money. In order for the businesses to be sustainable, they have to be profitable. But Social VC does not require the same high rate of financial return because it is also seeking social and environmental returns.

Social VC investors are emerging from a number of different sources. One is the corporate social responsibility area of public companies such as The Shell Foundation. The Shell Foundation is an independent UK based charity set up in 2000 and applies a 'business or enterprise-based approach to deliver self-financing solutions with measurable social benefits that can be replicated to achieve large scale impact'. At present it is involved in supporting start-ups and SME growth in Africa, reducing indoor air pollution and easing traffic congestion and pollution in large cities.

Kurt Hoffman, the director of The Shell Foundation, has explained his approach to business and enterprise based solutions as follows:

> We think programmes are more likely to be sustainable if people are treated as customers – not victims. Through our work – and partners – we try to find ways to give people what they want at an affordable price. This requires creativity and an entrepreneurial spirit. In other words, we try and 'inject business-DNA' into all of our programmes. We expect our partners to think and act like businesses. If they struggle then we help them to do this. Admittedly, this approach challenges some of the traditional development community. During the 2005 Make Poverty History campaign we argued – in our highly acclaimed report Enterprise Solutions to Poverty – that jobs and economic growth should be at the heart of the war on poverty, not aid and debt relief.

Other sources of funds are successful entrepreneurs and high net worth individuals who are interested in philanthropy and are prepared to allocate a small percentage of their total portfolio to this form of investment. Foundations and financial institutions are also beginning to engage in Social VC investment. The Omidyar Network was formed in 2004 by Pierre Omidyar (the founder of eBay) and his wife. The network has invested in a series of not- for-profit ventures as well as for-profits in line with the focus and values on which eBay was founded. These include inter-alia a variety of micro-finance institutions, financial institutions in South-East Europe which invest in developing SME's, a company producing solar electric light and a variety of web-based networks in a variety of fields.

Another example is Google.org, the philanthropic arm of Google that includes the work of The Google Foundation, which has made a number of investments which are Social VC projects. One is a non-profit venture fund that invests in market based solutions to global poverty in developing affordable goods and services to the 4 billion people who live on less that US $4 dollars a day. Another is an investment in Technoserve which helps entrepreneurs turn ideas into business: at present they are launching an entrepreneurship programme in Ghana. They are also involved in improving rural water supplies in Kenya and literacy in India through sub-titling Bollywood films and videos of popular folk songs.

Larger again would be the decisions by Citigroup in early 2007 to invest US $100 million alongside US $100 million invested by CDC, which is owned by the UK government and was formerly the Commonwealth Development Corporation. Citigroup is the most well-known private name to invest private equity in Africa, which in the past has been dominated by quasi- governmental development corporations such as CDC. This new Africa fund plans to make individual investments of US $20 – 60 million in sections such as telecoms, energy, transportation, consumer goods and natural resources.

Main stream investment funds are also beginning to allocate capital to this area. Legatum Global Partner (www.legatum.com) is an arm of Legatum Capital that invests in 'for-profit enterprises that provide a combination of financial and social returns on investments.' They are a 'double bottom line' investor and have focused particularly on companies in microfinance technologies that can reduce the cost of credit to the poor. Springhill Management (www.springhilluk.com), a biotech venture capital company, has been investing in this area for nine years. The Transformational Business Network (www.tbnetwork.org) has also recently created a US $1 million SME fund for Kenya.

The Importance of Small and Medium-sized Enterprises (SME's)

Most businesses fail because they are too small and under-capitalised. SME's that are properly capitalised and managed tend to have a higher rate of success because they are a:

Source of entrepreneurship and innovation:

SMEs provide an ideal environment for training in all aspects of business and also a place where new entrepreneurs can be groomed. Seventy five percent of all new businesses are started by people who have been previously employed in another company. In the developed countries SMEs are also known as innovative because of their quick response to market demands.

Driver of competition:

SMEs drive competition usually through their greater numbers. Competition in turn will drive innovation leading to new business start-ups.

The Small and Medium-sized Enterprise is the next step up from microfinance. It offers the advantages of scale and size to create more jobs, raises the success rate and provides the environment for on-the-job training and learning, even if it is via osmosis. The merits of this approach deserve further analysis.

First, it makes sense. Investing in sustainable businesses creates employment in the developing world. Real employment gives people the dignity and self-determinism to transform their own communities. This is in contrast to the dependency culture often engendered by aid. The strategy is to provide a 'hand-up not a hand-out' in order to alleviate poverty. Is it a surprise that poverty is linked to unemployment? *What the poor want is not aid, but jobs* – real jobs, not subsidised ones. This is the dignity and self- reliance they deserve.

One of the problems with aid is the need to keep asking donors for repeated support. In many cases donor fatigue eventually sets in. With social venture capital, funds can be provided either as equity investment or loan. *Donors become investors.* And we all know that investors are more likely to take an interest in their investments than donors will be in following up their gifts.

Second, encouraging the growth of SME's has worked before. Thirty years ago, the South East Asian countries were economic nobodies, their economies based on low priced commodities. Then Japanese companies started setting up manufacturing plants and were welcomed with open arms by the Asian governments. Why? Because they provided jobs for their people as well as training them in new technologies. Within a few years, enterprising Asians, trained by the Japanese began starting their own plants, often in competition with their 'masters'. The rest is history. Today the largest chip manufacturers are in Taiwan, Singapore and Malaysia – all locally owned. This is the Asian Tiger model. Whilst the Japanese companies did not have a social transformational agenda when they invested in Asia, nevertheless their investments demonstrate powerfully *how enterprise can alleviate poverty*. The key to reducing global poverty is economic growth. The most dramatic examples of this in recent years have been China and India. We are seeing China emerging from being a developing country to join the league of developed nations. This time it is through the Foreign Direct Investment (FDI) of companies from the United States, European Union and other Asian countries. If it has worked in Asia, it can also work in Africa. Sadly, Africa with 12% of the world's population has only 1% of global trade. In 2001, only 1.4% of global FDI went to Africa. Strip away oil investments and this reduces to zero. Africa cannot transform itself over any reasonable time frame without foreign investment.

We propose that social venture capital be regarded as a new asset class of investments. This will be attractive to high net worth entrepreneurs and the venture philanthropists who have always wanted to see venture capital principles and accountability in their philanthropic ´ ´ing. But it is equally attractive to institutions and foundations which have a Socially Responsible Investment (SRI) charter. Social venture capital can be structured in limited partnerships in exactly the same way as classical venture capital firms. Perhaps to compensate for a sub-venture capital rate of return, there can be tax benefits to encourage investments in this new asset class. A small portion of money for aid can also be channelled into social venture capital on a matched funding basis providing those who wish to set up this form of investment access to government funds.

The role of venture capital in developing new industries, such as IT and biotechnology, is well recognised. In the early days of an emerging industry, venture capital funds are needed to invest in high risk ventures in return for high returns. Financing options from banks and other financial institutions are unsuitable for these early stage companies because of the nature of the risks. In much the same way, investing in SMEs in developing countries carries a higher risk than normal businesses. We therefore believe that social venture capital is a more appropriate form of funding for these types of companies.

CHAPTER 6

Case studies from Africa, India and East Asia

The following are a selection of case studies of social venture capital.

Kuzuko Game Reserve, South Africa

Kuzuko Game Reserve, South Africa (www.legacyhotels.co.za, www.springhilluk.com, www.kuzuko.com) is a 39,000 acre game reserve situated adjacent to Addo Elephant Park (second largest after Kruger National Park) in a malaria-free zone. Its partner is the South Africa National Parks (SANP). The land is now fenced and disease-free animals indigenous to the region are being staged released by SANP. It will offer a safari experience to tourists in a 5-star lodge managed by Legacy Hotels, a leading hotel group in Southern Africa. It will employ 100 people directly when it opens in Q3 2007.

The project combines conservation, job creation and social transformation in a region of 70% adult unemployment. Other local partners include a number of financial agencies such as the Disability Employment Concern Trust (DECT), South African Development Bank (DBSA) and the Eastern Cape Development Corporation (ECDC). A Workers Trust has been created to enable employees to become shareholders in the business. The UK Foreign Office seconded an officer for a year to see first hand the project take shape. With their support, new commercially-viable business opportunities are currently being assessed with the aim of creating further jobs in the area.

The Eastern Cape Province is the poorest province in South Africa with a regional unemployment rate of 70%. Kuzuko is located in the Blue Crane Route Municipality (BCRM) which comprises three towns namely Somerset-East, Cookhouse and Pearston in the Eastern Cape. The main source of income from this region is from agriculture. BCRM has a total population of 54,000 people. Estimated adult unemployment is 87% with household income in 1999 – 2000 of R83 per week, equivalent to around US $2 per day per household. Assuming an average household of 4 people, this amounts to one-half US dollar per person per day. The area has all the social problems associated with high unemployment including a 20% HIV infection.

Given the depressed social conditions, Kuzuko was set up as a project to stimulate economic activities in the region. Over a 5-year period, the following impact has been achieved:

Economic impact:
- Employment for a core staff of 30 on the game reserve, most of whom had never been permanently employed before.
- Seventy men employed to fence around 70 miles over a 9 month period. These men were subsequently assisted to form their own fencing business.
- Thirty men plus sub-contractors employed to build 10 staff housing.
- Seventy men plus sub-contractors employed to build the main lodge.

According to the mayor of BCRM, Kuzuko has been the most significant contributor to the economy of the district over the past few years. Kuzuko together with the Addo Elephant Park, are attracting other economic activities into the area including tourism related businesses such as bed-and- breakfast lodging. BCRM has also recently committed to building an airport in Somerset East to be opened in 2007. This airport will open up the district to further economic development.

Eco-tourism is the fastest growth industry in this area and Kuzuko has been a catalyst in this process. It has been estimated that every 10 foreign tourist creates one local job. Assuming a minimum of 100 tourists per week at Kuzuko, this translates to over 500 jobs a year. Kuzuko expects to continue being a major catalyst for job creation in the coming years. In addition, Kuzuko's management team will also be involved in the starting of new enterprises with its local partners in the areas of agriculture, bio-fuel, laundry, waste management and building maintenance.

Social Impact:
- Wages paid by Kuzuko are substantially higher than the minimum wage (R35 per day) in neighbouring farms.
- R3.5m has been invested in 21 houses with inside bathroom and toilets, hot and cold water and free services. The standard of housing is well above farm labourer or government urban housing for the poor.
- Staff receive training in a variety of areas including driving lessons, vehicle maintenance, building skills, fencing and electric fence maintenance, game guards and conservation.
- Staff hold shares in the business giving them a stake in profits and encouraging interest in the venture. In addition, staff are encouraged to build up capital through savings and a number have bought cattle that graze on adjoining fields.
- For the first time, in many cases, staff have contracts, disability and life insurance, unemployment cover and workmen's compensation. Staff are informed of their working conditions and rights.
- Staff also receive guidance on life skills and HIV-Aids prevention. Counselling and rehab initiation facilities are available for those with alcohol dependency.

Environmental impact:
- Kuzuko has rehabilitated 39,000 acres of land previously used for stock farming, and have incorporated it into the 1.2 m acre Addo Elephant Park.
- It is running conservation programmes with its partner, SANP for the black rhino, elephant and wild dog.
- The first black rhinos and elephants to graze the karoo in 150 years have now been released.

The Kuzuko project has drawn much local support including that of Mr Mzwandile Mjadu, the mayor of the BCRM:

> We are delighted with the new Kuzuko Game Reserve which is assisting our community to gain new skills and employment. It is also acting as a catalyst to attract other investors and major funding institutions to our rural area. This is no small achievement in an isolated impoverished area. Thank you for being a catalyst for social transformation.

SPOT Taxis, Bangalore, India

SPOT Taxis is the largest taxi franchise in Bangalore with over 300 taxis and operates 24/7. This is the first commercial radio taxi operator in India and was started for social reasons in 1999, in particular to encourage the unemployed to seek employment and for drivers to become owners. One unique feature is that each driver is enabled to own his own vehicle with a structured loan over a 3 – 4 year period. They all have in-car radios and are directed by a control room using a computer system which tracks their location. This way, drivers make their money based on shorter pick-up routes and longer drop-off points.

SPOT stands for Self Employment Programme for Organised Transport. It has a corporate entity that structures the loans for the vehicles, equips them with radios to a uniformly high standard, operates the control room, trains and provides legal and ancillary support to the drivers. Through the corporate entity, it is able to negotiate vehicle leases with major banks like ICICI on behalf of the drivers most of whom have no credit history and would not have access to credit on their own. Because of its buying power, it has strategic alliances with Maruti Udyog Ltd for vehicles, Pulsar Inc for the electronic meters and Motorola for radios.

SPOT combines the management and financial strengths of a corporate entity with the entrepreneur vigour of self-employment.

Unlike other operators, SPOT's fleet are driven by owners who operate as individual businesses linked by a common brand, system, processes and values. This, coupled with their reliability and high quality service, differentiates them from other taxi operators.

Each driver takes on a Rs 60,000 loan. They make the monthly loan repayment as well as pay a management fee to the corporate entity for its centralised services. Average monthly earning per vehicle is around Rs 25,500. Fuel and maintenance amount to Rs 10,000 and the loan repayment plus management fee is around Rs 8,000. Each owner driver therefore is able to earn around Rs 7,000 per month. The attraction of owning a business within such a franchise has drawn people from all backgrounds and caste so that SPOT's drivers include ex-civil servants, security guards, police constables and the rural unemployed. It has been found that by running their own businesses, drivers are more motivated with the result that productivity is increased. In fact some enterprising drivers now own more than one vehicle. In addition to its attraction of helping the poor to own their businesses and build a credit history, this is a model which is easy to replicate.

Brains Group, UK and Moldova

Brains Group, (www.brainsdirect.com), is a software outsourcing business. The company offers IT consulting, development, support, delivery and outsourcing services to clients worldwide. The marketing office is in the UK but the software engineers are based in Moldova, one of the smallest and poorest countries in Eastern Europe, which employs over 150 technical staff. These employees are taught new skills, are learning about how businesses are run and are taught integrity. The taxes they pay represent a significant percentage of the total tax revenue of Moldova with a population of about 4 million people.

Brains Group was founded in 2000 and started offering its services to European clients from its first Development Centre in Chisinau, Moldova.

A second Development Centre opened in Bucharest, Romania in 2004 and currently employs 50 software engineers. One of the foundational principles of The Brains Group is what the company calls, the '3-way win'. They are committed to achieving leadership in IT sourcing by offering genuine win-win solutions to their clients, themselves and the countries that they operate in. They have a distinct set of values and approach:

Throughout our operations we aim to use the highest standards of ethical business practice, and seek to treat all of our stakeholders as well as we would expect them to treat us.

Supporting these values, the Brains Group is an active supporter of the Compudava Foundation (www.compudavafoundation. org). Founded in Moldova by the Brains Group, the Compudava Foundation is a not-for-profit organisation designed to contribute to sustainable development within the Republic of Moldova through supporting the advance of ICT via two primary areas of need: education and health.

The Brains Group is committed to using business to bring positive transformation to the countries that we work in. We made the strategic decision to source the majority of our requirements from Moldova because of the strength, depth and motivation of the local IT talent and because it gives us an ability to help improve the local economic situation. In supporting The Brains Group you help us to make a tangible difference to the people of Europe's poorest economy.

This is an ethical and quality business that is about more than providing a financial return to investors. Its business activities have already brought positive transformation to Moldova. To date, Compudava Foundation, the charity supported by Brains Group has been able to source and supply over 10,000 computers to schools and hospitals in the country.

Hagar Project, Cambodia

Hagar Project's (www.hagarproject.com) stated mission is 'To foster hope for vulnerable women and children in crisis through holistic, transformational development and creative initiatives.' Hagar was founded in response to the problems of street mothers and children in post conflict Cambodia. It takes in women who have been abused and raped during the Khmer war, rehabilitates them through a programme of counselling and then trains them to work in their growing number of businesses.

To break the cycle of violence and poverty in Cambodia, Hagar believes in an integrated three-pronged approach of rehabilitation, prevention and reintegration.

Rehabilitation, or providing the vulnerable mothers and children with the necessary life skills and income-earning capacities to transform their lives through a temporary home; counselling; literacy, numeracy, and health and nutrition training, vocational skills training; schooling and day care.

Prevention, or instituting interventions that will stave off women's downward slide into destitution such as training in literacy and numeracy, income earning skills, children's and women's rights and job placement. All education promotes community health (including HIV/AIDS), empowerment, human rights, anti-trafficking and anti-domestic violence agendas.

Reintegration, where the mothers and their children are re-established in mainstream society through livelihood opportunities in agriculture, self employment, garment sewing or in Hagar's micro-businesses.

Hagar owns and operates a number of commercial enterprises:
- *Hagar Design:* Produces women's accessories and home furnishings of fine hand woven silk and other fabrics for export and tourist markets.
- *Hagar Soya:* Operates a modern beverage facility and markets nutritious soya milk in Cambodia.

- *Hagar Catering:* Provides nutritious meals to city workers through a meal catering service in hotels and factories and runs a facility cleaning service. This business now caters to the Inter-Continental Hotel as well as the US Embassy. It recently turned cash flow positive and has been able to plough its profits back into its charitable activities.

Since 1994, Hagar has helped around 100,000 mothers, children and family members through its social programs and economic projects. Although funded by charitable organisations and governments, it is seeking to be self- funding with profits from its commercialised ventures. This is a holistic approach to tackling the problem of street mothers and children. What is exciting about this model is the restoration of dignity to these abused women through their rehabilitation and employment.

Lessons from Social Venture Capital Cases

What is common about these projects? Each was started as a social venture capital business by an entrepreneur with the vision and the courage to take the risks. Funds were introduced into the businesses either as equity investments or as loans. The businesses operate in the mainstream and are run commercially. The employees understand that they are not working for a charity. Their long term employment is dependent on the success of the companies. Just as the Japanese FDI spawned new local entrepreneurs in Asia, so these projects expect to train and spawn the next generation of entrepreneurs in their countries. These projects help the poor with both employment as well as capital building – job creation and wealth creation. In our experience, helping the poor build capital, either intellectual (through education and skills training) or asset (ownership of a taxi, a cow or share equity), is critical to poverty alleviation.

And the cities of the developing countries are teeming with entrepreneurs who are creative, enthusiastic and resourceful. But like entrepreneurs everywhere they need access to capital and credit to start their businesses. C.K. Prahalad has estimated that the market at the 'bottom of the pyramid' based on people living on less than $2 a day, is worth $13 trillion a year. Whilst he is encouraging the multinational firms to address this market, we believe it will be more effectively tackled by local entrepreneurs through their SMEs. Social VC builds businesses at the 'bottom of the pyramid' that have the ability to move up the pyramid into the main stream.

But social venture capital is a tough business. It requires business expertise and courage. It is riskier than a development project. Trying to get businesses going in the developed countries, with good access to capital and support infrastructures is difficult enough. It will be much tougher 'out there'. There will be failures. But even in failures, people learn new skills and diehard entrepreneurs will try again and again until they succeed. In the USA, they call those who have failed in a couple of ventures 'experienced'. Starting and running businesses requires different kinds of skills to those present in the NGO community. Government funding for social enterprise should seek out the social venture capital organisations, including the faith-based ones, to administer such funds for business ventures.

For social venture capital projects to succeed, several factors need to be present. There needs to be trusted and experienced local management in place. As with normal businesses, partnerships with other companies and institutions to secure technical expertise and additional management support are important. Partnerships also limit the risks of the businesses. Many of these social venture capital projects leverage local funding by acting as the lead investor syndicating other investors, soft loans and grants from government and development agencies. This kind of financial leveraging further reduces risks. Local funding often only happens as matched funding when there is a demonstrable FDI in place. Local funding also means local ownership which further improves the chances of success for the business. In most cases, these businesses empower the management and employees with some ownership of their business.

The single biggest requirement for FDI is investor confidence in the macro-economic policy and stability of the country. Transparency, good governance and effective legal system are all necessities for attracting investments. However, it is in this very area of creating an environment that fosters business start ups that the developing countries are the weakest. The World Bank's report *Doing Business* in 2006, shows that it takes 17 procedures and 165 days to start a business in Congo Democratic Republic compared with just 2 procedure and 2 days in Australia. For export of goods, it takes 16 documents and 60 days in Zambia compared with the 3 documents and 6 days in Denmark. Incredibly the export documents for Zambia require 25 different signatories. Still this is better than the record- breaking 45 signatories needed in the Congo Democratic Republic. This kind of inefficient bureaucracy encourages corruption and discourages entrepreneurship. In fact the World Bank suggests that future funding should be made 'conditional on cutting the time and cost of business start-up.' This proposal, using the research of Hernando de Soto, is designed to foster private enterprise. He contends for example that giving Africans secure title to their property would encourage private enterprise which would by itself triple the annual income of the whole continent.

CHAPTER 7

The way forward

We believe that tackling world poverty must be a major priority for our time. The poverty, hunger, disease, lack of schooling, water and housing is a reproach to our generation. Increasing aid is of value and we welcome in particular the commitments which have been made on immunisation, vaccination and the provision of schooling for all. But there is no evidence to show that aid will produce more rapid economic growth, create more jobs or reduce poverty. Aid is neither necessary nor sufficient to ensure sustainable development and poverty reduction in poor countries. Encouraging enterprise is vital to achieving these goals.

Micro finance has shown the way forward in removing people from abject poverty to 'normal' poverty. The next step is increased investment through small and medium sized companies in poor countries which yields both financial and social returns. The way forward therefore consists of a number of steps.

First, to encourage foundations, trusts, high net worth individuals and companies, through their social responsibility budgets, to invest in social venture capital projects rather than by simply making charitable donations.

Second, to encourage governments to devote a greater proportion of its aid budget to funding enterprise, and to design tax policies that promote social venture investments.

Third, to reduce trade barriers so that developing countries can increase both their exports and imports; if that fails, to encourage countries to unilaterally liberalise their trading agreements.

There are no easy answers to the eradication of poverty. There is no 'one size fits all' or a single solution. Poverty will ultimately be solved when good governments are installed that will create the environment for vibrant economic activity to take place. It will not be solved by grand projects run by governments but which offer poor returns on their investments. Enterprise based strategy will lay the groundwork for a better educated and resourced next generation, to transform their nations and make poverty history.

BIBLIOGRAPHY

Aid and Development. Will it work this time? (2005) Fredrik Erixon

'Aid, Policies and Growth', American Economic Review (2000)
C. Burnside & D. Dollar

Commercial Returns and Social Value: The Case of Microfinance,
Harvard Business School (2006) Michael Chu

Corruption and Foreign Aid in Africa, Foreign Policy Research Institute (2005)
H. Werlin

Doing Business in 2006, World Bank (2005)

Fifty Years of Failure, Centre for Policy Studies (1999) P. Bauer & C. Onslow

*Fostering sustainable complexity in the microfinance industry: Which way
forward?* Institute of Economic Affairs (2005) Emily Chamlee-Wright

*New Data, New Doubts: A comment on Burnside and Dollar's 'Aid,
Policies, and Growth' (2000),* Center for Global Development (2003)
W. Easterly, R. Levine & D. Roodman

*The Fortune at the Bottom of the Pyramid. Eradicating Poverty Through
Profits,* Wharton School Publishing (2004) C.K. Prahalad

The Mystery of Capital, Basic Books (2000) H. de Soto

Time to Stop Fooling Ourselves about Foreign Aid, Cato Institute (2005)
T. Dichter

*Voices of the Poor reports: Can anyone hear us? Crying out for change,
From many lands,* Oxford University Press (2000, 2000, 2002) Narayan,
Deepa (et al.)

World Bank Development Indicators, World Bank (2003)

United Nations Development Programme (2003)

ABOUT THE AUTHORS

BRIAN GRIFFITHS is Vice-Chairman of Goldman Sachs International and has been heavily involved in China since the early 1990s. Previously he taught at the London School of Economics, was Dean of the City University Business School, a director of the Bank of England and head of the Prime Minister's Policy Unit at 10 Downing Street from 1985 – 1990. He was made a life peer as Lord Griffiths of Fforestfach in 1991.

KIM TAN is the Chairman of SpringHill Management Ltd, a specialist venture capital management company in biotech and pharmaceutical investments. He is a Fellow of the Royal Society of Medicine, a board member of the Asia-Pacific Economic Community's (APEC) Life Sciences Forum, a board director of a number of companies in Malaysia, India, the European Union and the USA, and a founding director of the Transformational Business Network (TBN).

TBN (www.tbnetwork.org) is a network of business people and corporate organisations that uses an enterprise approach to tackle global poverty and bring social transformation. TBN supports commercially sustainable small-medium-size enterprises (SMEs) in developing countries that create jobs, empower the poor and transform communities. TBN members do this by contributing time and skills, mentoring developing entrepreneurs, and direct investments in emerging businesses. TBN was launched in March of 2003 and currently has 25 projects running that will create or support over 7500 jobs. Its goal is to create one million jobs.

Printed in Great Britain
by Amazon